Clever Word Search Puzzles for Kids

Mark Danna

PUZZLE
WRIGHT
PRESS

New York

For my dad, whose bad jokes and silly musical
sense of humor definitely left their mark

PUZZLE
WRIGHT
PRESS
New York

An Imprint of Sterling Publishing
387 Park Avenue South
New York, NY 10016

ISBN 978-1-4549-0969-9

Distributed in Canada by Sterling Publishing
C/o Canadian Manda Group, 165 Dufferin Street
Toronto, Ontario, Canada M6K 3H6
Distributed in the United Kingdom by GMC Distribution Services
Castle Place, 166 High Street, Lewes, East Sussex, England BN7 1XU
Distributed in Australia by Capricorn Link (Australia) Pty. Ltd.
P.O. Box 704, Windsor, NSW 2756, Australia

For information about custom editions, special sales, and premium and
corporate purchases, please contact Sterling Special Sales
at 800-805-5489 or specialsales@sterlingpublishing.com.

Manufactured in the United States of America

2   4   6   8   10   9   7   5   3   1

www.puzzlewright.com

Contents

Introduction
5

Puzzles
9

Word Lists
66

Answers
67

Index
94

Introduction

"Solving puzzles is an excellent way to exercise your brain while having fun at the same time." That's what Will Shortz, Puzzlemaster for National Public Radio, says, and he's right—especially about the very clever puzzles you'll find throughout this exceptionally entertaining book.

What makes these puzzles so clever? First off, the letters in every puzzle grid form a picture. So instead of the usual, ho-hum square or rectangle, you get lively shapes like a hockey goalie, a rearing horse, a chess king, a rocket ship, a teddy bear, a shamrock, the Empire State Building, a watering can, a windsurfer, a crescent moon, and a party balloon ... to name just a few. You get 53 puzzles in all—each one a visual treat, each one in a shape appropriate to the puzzle's theme.

To make things yet more interesting, we've added a few twists. In three puzzles, you'll need to build the word list from clues you're given. In "Animal Hunt," you'll hunt for words that contain the names of animals, like TOADstool. In "Mix and Match," you'll unscramble pairs of related words. In "The Game's Afoot," you'll try to figure out what the words are as well as what they have in common.

For even more variety, there are rebuses. In these puzzles, little pictures represent a set of letters inside the big picture. For example, in "Aw, Nuts!" every word or phrase in the word list contains the letters NUT in consecutive order. When these letters appear in the acorn-shaped grid, they appear as a 🌰. So the phrase IN A NUTSHELL in the word list would show up in the grid as INA🌰SHELL. In other rebus puzzles, you'll find little houses or little pans.

To top it all off, every puzzle contains a hidden message! After you've circled all the words and phrases in the grid, read all the uncircled letters from left to right, top to bottom, to spell out a silly quote, a fun fact, or the punch line to a "punny" riddle.

When you try to uncover the hidden message, the letters will be in order, but you'll need to figure out how to break them into words and where to add punctuation. That makes this puzzle-within-a-puzzle a real challenge and adds a level of difficulty not usually associated with word search puzzles. If you find it too hard, that's okay. You can get still get your laughs by reading the answers to the riddles in the answer section.

Finding the hidden messages may be tough, but learning to solve word searches is easy. If you know how to do them, you can jump in right now and get started. If you don't know how to do them, just keep on reading and we'll tell you everything you need to know.

What's a word search puzzle? A word search is a game of hide-and-seek: we hide the words; you go seek them. Each puzzle has two main parts: a grid and a word list. The grid looks like a meaningless jumble of letters, but it actually hides all the words and phrases in the word list. Most word search grids are rectangular or square—which is kind of boring—but in this book and in some others I've written, each grid comes in a distinctive picture shape that relates to the theme of the puzzle.

Words and phrases always go in a straight line—horizontally, vertically, or diagonally. Horizontal words go straight across to the right or backward to the left. Vertical words go straight down or straight up. Diagonal words slant from left-to-right or right-to-left and go either upward or downward along the angle. So words can go in eight possible directions—along the lines of a plus sign (+) or a multiplication sign (×).

What else should I know? In the grid, the same letter may be used in more than one word. This happens when words cross each other from two or more directions. You'll see lots of shared letters in this book because we've made sure that every word in a grid crosses at least one other word, and that all the words in a grid interconnect. It's a nice touch that's often missing elsewhere.

When you look for words and phrases in the grid, ignore all punctuation and spacing in the word list. For example, the phrase,

"DON'T DAWDLE!" in the word list would appear in the grid, in some direction, as DONTDAWDLE. Also, ignore all words in brackets like [THE] and [A]. These have been added at times to make certain word-list choices more understandable, but they will not appear in the grid.

How do I get started? Some people look for across words first. Others begin with the long words or ones with less common letters like Q, Z, X, or J. Still others start at the top of the list and work their way in order straight down to the bottom. Try a few ways and see what works best for you.

How do I mark the hidden words? Loop them, draw a straight line through them, or circle each individual letter. Whatever you choose, cross the words off the word list as you find them in the grid so as to avoid confusion. And be sure to be neat. Neatness will help when you're looking for all the letters that make up the hidden message.

What's in this book? There are 53 puzzles, each with a different shape and theme. Word lists generally contain 18 to 25 items. With a few exceptions, the puzzles are all about the same difficulty level, so feel free to jump around and do the puzzles in any order you like.

Any final words? The puzzle titles are playful, so don't be surprised if you're fooled at first as to what the puzzle theme is. And be prepared for a lot of good, silly fun in the hidden messages. Finally, have a great time from start to finish—from "Put On a Happy Face" and "Open for Business" straight through to "Start at the End" and "Let's Call It a Day."

—Mark Danna

1. PUT ON A HAPPY FACE

Shaped like a smiley face, the grid contains words and phrases associated with happiness and a positive attitude.

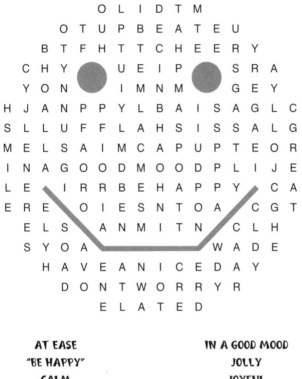

```
            O   L   I   D   T   M
        O   T   U   P   B   E   A   T   E   U
    B   T   F   H   T   T   C   H   E   E   R   Y
C   H   Y       U   E   I   P       S   R   A
Y   O   N       I   M   N   M       G   E   Y
H   J   A   N   P   P   Y   L   B   A   I   S   A   G   L   C
S   L   L   U   F   F   L   A   H   S   I   S   S   A   L   G
M   E   L   S   A   I   M   C   A   P   U   P   T   E   O   R
I   N   A   G   O   O   D   M   O   O   D   P   L   I   J   E
L   E   I   R   R   B   E   H   A   P   P   Y   C   A
E   R   E   O   I   E   S   N   T   O   A   C   G   T
    E   L   S   A   N   M   I   T   N   C   L   H
    S   Y   O   A   W   A   D   E
        H   A   V   E   A   N   I   C   E   D   A   Y
        D   O   N   T   W   O   R   R   Y   R
            E   L   A   T   E   D
```

AT EASE	IN A GOOD MOOD
"BE HAPPY"	JOLLY
CALM	JOYFUL
CHEERY	MERRY
CONFIDENT	OPTIMISTIC
"DON'T WORRY"	PHAT
EAGER	ROSY
ELATED	SERENE
GLAD	SMILE
"[THE] GLASS IS HALF FULL"	SUNNY
"GREAT!"	THUMBS-UP
GRIN	UPBEAT
"HAVE A NICE DAY"	

2. OPEN FOR BUSINESS

Shaped like a can of worms, the grid contains things you open. To open a can of worms is to bring up something that is best left unsaid. The hidden message answers the question, "Who should be the only ones to open a can of worms?"

```
        P                       E  D
        O  C  A  R  D           O
                 N     T  O  P        L
  C  L  A  S  P     U     R           E
  R        R        O     E     E  T  A  G
  A        E        W     A     F
  T     K  W  S  H  O  D  L  S  O  A  N
  E     O  E  E  D  E  L  P  U  R  S  E
        O  D  N  B  E  O  M  R  E  A  A
        B  I  T  R  F  O  I  E  G  T  J
        W  O  B  S  U  I  T  C  A  S  E
        F  M  X  T  S  L  L  H  C  D  O
        U  R  H  E  P  O  L  E  V  N  E
        F  I  Y  S  S  C  H  S  I  I  N
        E  J  A  C  K  E  T  G  M
```

BOOK	JARS
BOXES	LOCK
CAGE	[YOUR] MIND
CARD	[YOUR] MOUTH
CLASP	[AN] OLD WOUND
CRATE	PRESENT
DOOR	PURSE
ENVELOPE	SAFE
[YOUR] EYES	SUITCASE
FILE	TREASURE CHEST
GATE	UMBRELLA
JACKET	WINDOW

3. WHAT AN ICE GAME

Shaped like a hockey goalie, the grid contains words and phrases about hockey. The hidden message is a scary fact about the early decades of the sport.

```
                K   K   I
                N   C   T
            H   I   I   I   E
            N   R   T   G   R   S
        G   O   S   S   H   O   T
        E   N   I   L   A   L   D   A   T
I       E   S   Z   A   M   B   O   N   I   A   D
  D       S   S   I   D   A   L   W   I   L       N   H   T
    E   T   A   K   S   S   A   H   I   R   E       W   E   A
        F   V       K   D   I       N   E   Y
        R   E       E   S   A       G   P   C
            N   T   S           F   U   H
            L   S   A           C   P   C
        E   A   E   E           M   N   K
        P   O   A       M       S   E   K
            G           A           B
                E   N   O   Z
```

ASSIST	PUCK
BENCH	RINK
BLADE	SAVE
DEFENSEMAN	SHOT
GOAL	SKATE
HAT TRICK	STANLEY CUP
ICING	STICK
LINE	WHISTLE
MASK	WING
PASS	ZAMBONI
PERIOD	ZONE

4. PLUG IT IN

Shaped like a plug, the grid contains things you plug in. The hidden message answers the riddle, "What happened to the boy who got it backwards when he was told to take a little plug?"

```
          H  N  D
          E  R  O
       T  Y  E  O  R
    T  E  S  V  T  E  I
    R  O  P  A  K  T  A
 P  E  S  M  W  B  N  I  C
 M  N  G  A  O  G  I  O  L
 A  O  S  U  R  L  R  E  O
F L H  D  P  C  D  P  R  C  I
N E P  S  E  I  T  E  E  K  A
R D O  C  O  M  P  U  T  E  R
    R              S
    C              A
    I              O
    M              T
```

AMPS	MICROPHONE
CLOCK	MICROWAVE
COMPUTER	MODEM
CORD	PRINTER
DRYER	STEREO
FANS	TOASTER
IRON	TV SET
LAMP	WASHER

5. I NEED THIS RIDE NOW!

Shaped like a horse, the grid contains things you ride, ride in, or ride on. The hidden message is something you ride that takes you right back to where you started.

```
        P A M
      F R O O
  C A M E L N N
      O L R O Y
      O G R L
    I A M A I
    W X E I V S
    R B A L L A W
  S C O O T E R N H C
  T     Y A W B U S E S
  E         T R O L L E Y
  J         O A E K     L
    S       D I       U
            B G       G
            T H       E
          E R
```

BIKE	PONY
BOAT	SCOOTER
BUSES	SLED
CAMEL	SLEIGH
FERRIS WHEEL	SUBWAY
JETS	TAXI
LIMO	TROLLEY
LUGE	VANS
MONORAIL	WAGON

6. NEW YORK, NEW YORK

Shaped like the top part of the Empire State Building, the grid contains words and phrases associated with New York City. The hidden message is a fact that begins, "Because New York has so much going on all of the time ..."

```
                        Y
                        T
                        R
                        E
                        B
                    I   I   M
                B   I   L   E   D
            S   T   R   F   L   T   E
            C   E   S   O   R   R   S
        S   C   O   E   S   E   A   M   U   M   F
        O   K   N   R   N   U   H   D   B   L   E
        S   M   A   T   Q   T   B   Y   W   C   R
        Y   U   A   S   L   A   R   L   A   A   R
        C   S   S   L   E   T   D   A   Y   T   Y
    I   H   A   E   E   L   C   S   I   P   L   O   H   O   S
    X   T   M   U   F   A   S   H   I   O   N   P   Y   P   T
    A   I   H   M   A   W   T   Z   N   E   V   E   A   R
    T   S   L   S   E   E   Z   O   O   Z   X   N   O   R   B
    P   S   R   E   P   A   R   C   S   Y   K   S   S   A   K
```

BROADWAY	OPERA
BRONX ZOO	PIZZA
BUSES	SAKS
CENTRAL PARK	SKYSCRAPERS
DELI	SOHO
FASHION	STATUE OF LIBERTY
FERRY	SUBWAY
HARLEM	TAXI
MACY'S	TIMES SQUARE
MUSEUMS	WALL STREET

7. AW, NUTS!

Every item in the word list contains the letters NUT in consecutive order. When these letters appear in the acorn-shaped grid, they have been replaced by a 🌰. We hope this puzzle doesn't drive you 🌰S. The hidden message completes the sentence, "Nuts are often a healthy food, so ..."

```
                  H
🌰 🌰 S 🌰 D E T S A O R L I T B
 S T L O B D N A S 🌰 L M H R A
   K Y A E S S U E E N A S
     E P W T H Q H A V Z Z
     🌰 N R L A S T M I 🌰 E
     C O C O 🌰 🌰 T L 🌰 C L
     A I N A F R 🌰 U I R 🌰
     S T N 🌰 A E P R M A T
     E I I G S T S I I C N
     N R U U T T R S D K G
       🌰 I L T U I O O E
       N W O R B 🌰 O M R
         C H E S T 🌰 U
             S
```

BRAZIL NUT
BUTTERNUT SQUASH
CHESTNUT
COCONUT
DIMINUTIVE
DONUTS
HAZELNUT
IN A NUTSHELL
LAST-MINUTE
LUG NUT

MR. PEANUT
NUT-BROWN
NUTCASE
"[THE] NUTCRACKER"
NUTMEG
NUTRITION
NUTS AND BOLTS
"[THE] NUTTY PROFESSOR"
ROASTED NUTS
WALNUT

8. LOSER!

Shaped like a key, the grid contains things you might lose. The hidden message answers the riddle, "What happened to the boy who got bored and took all the money out of his savings account?"

```
        E  M  A  G
     T  U  R  N  L  C
  H  I  E        A  O  L
  W  M  P  P  F  S  M  A
  O  E  R  I  A  S  B  C
  D  S  I  R  I  E  A  R
     N  V  G  T  S  E
        I  T  H  W
        L  M  O  T
     R  E  P  M  E  T
        G  I  N  S
        E  K  U
        S  R
        T  O  T
        E  W
        K  E  Y  S
        R  M  E
        H  O  P  E
        S  H  T
```

A BET	KEYS
CASH	[YOUR] MIND
COMB	POWER
FAITH	PRIVILEGES
GAME	[YOUR] TEMPER
GLASSES	TIME
[YOUR] GRIP	TRUST
[YOUR] HOMEWORK	[YOUR] TURN
HOPE	WEIGHT

9. GET A LOAD OF THIS!

Shaped like a rocket ship, the grid carries a full payload of 25 items—24 in the word list and one in the hidden message. Each item is made from letters that appear in the phrase ROCKET SHIP. (Note: no letter is ever repeated within a word.) When you're done with the puzzle, try a different game: see how many more words you can make from the letters in ROCKET SHIP. One final thought ... in the hidden message, the ROCKET SHIP turns into a certain make of car.

```
                    R
                 E  E  P
                 S  K  O
              T  R  O  P  S
              T  O  P  O  E
              S  H  R  E  K
              E  H  I  T  O
              I  C  O  I  H
              K  R  H  C  C
              C  T  C  O  K
              O  T  R  C  P
              R  S  R  I  S
              I  H  T  O  C
           C  C  C  R  R  P  E
        K  T  H  R  O  E  I  H  P
     E  E  E  E  O  C  H  T  C  I  S
  R  K  R     S  P  S  C  H     H  E  H
  S  S  T     T  S  E  R  C     C  E  S
```

CHIP	OSTRICH	SHOCK
CHOIR	PITCHERS	SHREK
CHOKE	PITH	SICKER
CREST	POETIC	SKETCH
ECHO	POKER	SPORT
ESCORT	PORCH	TREK
HEROIC	RICHEST	TRICEPS
HORSE	ROCKIEST	TROPHIES

17

10. LISTEN UP

Shaped like a bell, the grid contains things you hear or listen to. The hidden message completes the joke, "Do you know the smartest kid in class is going deaf?"

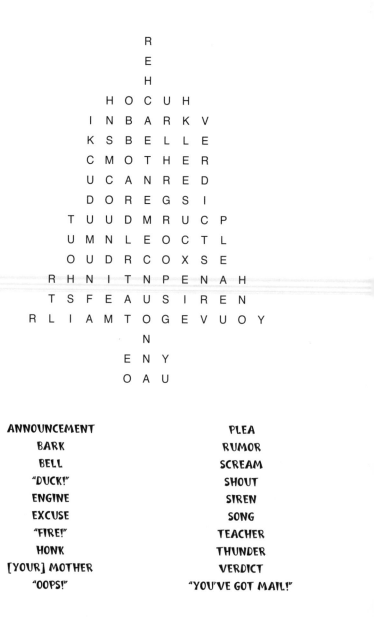

```
                    R
                    E
                    H
            H  O  C  U  H
         I  N  B  A  R  K  V
         K  S  B  E  L  L  E
         C  M  O  T  H  E  R
         U  C  A  N  R  E  D
         D  O  R  E  G  S  I
   T  U  U  D  M  R  U  C  P
   U  M  N  L  E  O  C  T  L
   O  U  D  R  C  O  X  S  E
R  H  N  I  T  N  P  E  N  A  H
   T  S  F  E  A  U  S  I  R  E  N
R  L  I  A  M  T  O  G  E  V  U  O  Y
                    N
                 E  N  Y
                 O  A  U
```

ANNOUNCEMENT	PLEA
BARK	RUMOR
BELL	SCREAM
"DUCK!"	SHOUT
ENGINE	SIREN
EXCUSE	SONG
"FIRE!"	TEACHER
HONK	THUNDER
[YOUR] MOTHER	VERDICT
"OOPS!"	"YOU'VE GOT MAIL!"

11. ON THE GO

Shaped like a beach umbrella, the grid contains places and things you might go to. The hidden message tells what could happen to you in a game of Monopoly.

```
                        M
                P P Y O O P N
            O U A I T O A V M W I
            S R G R E R H S I T O
        G T R O C K C O N C E R T
        Y O P S S L E E P H H S O
    L D R I S L R D E S U C O C T
    I I E M A G L L A B R L A O Y
    A T   M L O   R   G C O   E L
    J     C     O     H       B
                W
                Y
                E
                N
                S
                I
                D
```

AIRPORT	PARK
BALL GAME	PARTY
BEACH	PIECES
CHURCH	ROCK CONCERT
CLASS	[YOUR] ROOM
DISNEY WORLD	SCHOOL
JAIL	SLEEP
MALL	STORE
MOVIES	TOWN

12. SOFT IN THE HEAD

Shaped like a teddy bear, the grid contains things that are or may be soft. The hidden message tells you the famous person for whom the teddy bear was named.

```
            P  R  E
         G  N  I  D  N  A  L
         S  I  ●  I  ●  T  L
            S  K  ●  E  A
            S  U  D  O  D
            D  C  S
         R  Y  D  O  O  L  W  E
      R  A  B  B  I  T  S  F  O  O  T
   N  I  E     W  A  T  E  R     P  L  T
   N  A        O  A  O  T  E     D  E  G
   R  H     B  L  A  N  K  E  T
            J  L  D  T  G  Y  R
            O  I  O  P  A  O  S
      O  O  B  P        S  R  E  V
      K  I  S  S        E  L  A  T
```

ANGORA	LANDING
BLANKET	PILLOW
COAL	RABBIT'S FOOT
COTTON	RAIN
DATA	SKIN
FOCUS	SLOPE
GLOW	SOAP
HAIR	SPOT
JOBS	TEDDY BEAR
KISS	WATER

13. THREW AND THREW

Shaped like a die used in games of chance, the grid contains things you throw. The hidden message is a word of advice.

```
                  J  U  P  S  U  P  P  O  R  T
               E  E  B  S  I  R  F  P  D     I
            D  C  O  O  ●  O  T  E  I  A  P  F
         P  N  N  O  O  N  E  N  C     F  S  Y
      G  A  M  E  T  M  S  A  E  I  H  O  C  S
   R  L     E  P     E  L        O  ●  O  I  S
   G  ●  K  U  O  T  R  E  ●     V  N  T  S  I
   M  S  N  O  W  B  A  L  L  A  F  L  B  T  H
   H  C  T  L  O  P  N  N  R  E  O  B  A  ●  L
   H  C  Y  O  D  E  G  M  T     S  L  L  D  O
   N  T  T  A  N  L  E  T  K  R  L  T  L  T
   H  E  R  I  I  E  I  I  A  A  U  A  M
   T  T  A  H  W  R  S  E  W     S  M
   S  ●  P  O  W  S  P  A  ●  S  Y
   D  I  S  C  U  S  Y  O  O  U
```

BOOMERANG	GLANCE	SNOWBALL
CONFETTI	HISSY FIT	SPEAR
DARTS	IT ALL AWAY	STONES
DICE	KISS	SUPPORT
DISCUS	LASSO	SWITCH
FOOTBALL	PARTY	TANTRUM
FRISBEE	PASS	VOICE
GAME	PITCH	WINDOW OPEN
	PUNCH	

14. ANIMAL HUNT

Shaped like a toadstool, the grid features 18 words and phrases that contain the names of animals, like TOADstool. But like many real animals, these animals are shy and in hiding. Before you try to hunt them in the grid, use the crossword-style clues on this page to spot the words and phrases they're hiding in. The blanks tell you the number of letters in each animal's name, and the word list, when correctly filled in, will be in alphabetical order. Each entire word or phrase, not just the animal, will appear in the grid on the opposite page. If you need help, you can turn to the word list on page 66. The hidden message is a goofy sentence containing three more animal phrases.

1. Tumbler at a circus
A C R O _ _ _

2. Avid reader
B O O K _ _ _ _

3. Short snooze
_ _ _ N A P

4. Tuft of hair sticking up
_ _ _ L I C K

5. Tool used to pry open a door
_ _ _ _ B A R

6. Not seeming quite on the up and up
_ _ _ _ Y

7. Advertising handout
_ _ _ E R

8. Raised flesh from fear or cold, or R. L. Stine series
_ _ _ _ _ B U M P S

9. Frankfurter
H O T _ _ _

10. Kids' jumping game
L E A P _ _ _ _

11. The largest portion
_ _ _ _ ' S S H A R E

12. Be more sly than
O U T _ _ _

13. Tight braids of hair
_ _ _ T A I L S

14. Tiring, competitive rush
_ _ _ R A C E

15. Zapper in some old sci-fi movies
_ _ _ G U N

16. Carpenter's frame for cutting wood
S A W _ _ _ _ _

17. Famous golfer
_ _ _ _ _ W O O D S

18. Poisonous mushroom
_ _ _ _ S T O O L

```
          O A S A
        U B A A T C
      B T O B Y W S K R H
    A F T O N O H A C E O C
  L O O T S D A O T I Y T B P
  X E N U G Y A R K L L D U A
S L I A T G I P S C W F O K N T
O O C S P M U B E S O O G L T O
C Y H S I F K L O E C A R T A R
C R O W B A R I T N F O X M C T
          O I
          N G
          S E
          S R
          H W
          A O
          R O
          E D
          V S
```

15. FLOATING AWAY

Shaped like a person windsurfing, the grid contains things that float on water. The hidden message completes the riddle, "Why did the boy put a canned soft drink in the bathtub with him?" "He wanted ..."

```
                        K
                        T  A
                        O  B  Y  E
        H  L  A         E  O  N  A  C
        V  I  E      A  R  I  A  F  K  N
           L      C  M  A  R  L  C  I  B
        E  Y  E  H  O  A  O  F  O  I  U  U
     J  A  P  B  O  R  O  I  T  L  G  O
     E  G  A  U  T  S  K  C  S  S  N  Y
     L  L  D  T     H  S  E  A  L  E  S
     L  A  E  R     M  T  B  M  I  P  N
     Y  R  B  E     A  E  E  E  O  A
     F     N        L  R  R  N  W
     I     N        L  O  G  S
     S     I        O  E
     H  F     L  O  W
  A  L  I  F  E  P  R  E  S  E  R  V  E  R  T
```

ALGAE	LILY PAD
BEACHBALL	LOGS
BUOYS	MARSHMALLOWS
CANOE	MINE
CORK	OIL SLICK
FLOTSAM	OTTER
ICEBERG	PENGUIN
INNER TUBE	RAFT
JELLYFISH	SEAL
KAYAK	SPONGE
LIFE PRESERVER	SWAN

16. IT'S A GIFT!

Shaped like a party balloon, the grid contains things kids might like to get for birthday gifts. The hidden message is a definition of a gifted child.

```
            A  M  K  I  D
         W  O  E  R  E  T  S
      C  N  A  M  K  L  A  W  H
   C  E  K  I  B  X  M  B  O  G  E
   Y  L  R  E  D  R  O  C  M  A  C
   T  L  O  S  B  O  O  K  A  L  O
   T  P  L  T  E  L  E  C  A  R  B
   O  H  T  O  H  L  A  P  T  O  P
   F  O  V  I  D  E  O  G  A  M  E
   P  N  S  R  E  R  S  E  O  H  S
      E  E  Y  O  B  E  M  A  G
         T  S  E  L  N  T  S
            C  H  A  R  M
               D
               E
               S
            D
         V
      D
```

BMX BIKE	GAMEBOY
BOOK	LAPTOP
BRACELET	MONEY
CAMCORDER	ROLLERBLADES
CELLPHONE	SHOES
CHARM	STEREO
CLOTHES	TV SET
DOLL	VIDEOGAME
DVDS	WALKMAN

17. TAKE FIVE

Shaped like the number 5, the grid contains 23 five-letter words that each begin with a different letter of the alphabet. The hidden message answers the question, "So who's missing?"

```
H  E  L  L  O  B  M  I  L  O
E  L  B  O  W  I  N  G  S  H
E  A  L
F  G  T
I  E  E
N  N  N
K  T  S  C  E  N  T  S
S  V  E  X  E  D  R  I  N  K
               A  O  O  Q
               I  T  U
               S  S  I
               Y  U  E
M  E  G              A  U  O  T
B  L  A  Z  E  B  R  A  Y  J
P  R  I  D  E  X  I  M
```

AGENT	NOISY
BLAZE	OWING
CENTS	PRIDE
DRINK	QUIET
ELBOW	RAISE
FENCE	SCENT
HELLO	TENSE
IGLOO	VEXED
JOUST	WINGS
KNIFE	X-RAYS
LIMBO	ZEBRA
MIXED	

18. PUT YOUR HOUSE IN ORDER

Here are the HOUSE RULES. Every item in the word list contains the letters HOUSE in consecutive order. When these letters appear in the house-shaped grid, they have been replaced by a 🏠. So make a 🏠PARTY out of this 🏠WORK because this puzzle is ON THE 🏠.

```
                          A
                  🏠  🏠  D     B  🏠
              H  O  T  🏠  L  H  🏠
           D  R  O  K  U  G  O  T
        O  E  🏠  T  R  U  O  C  H
     G  N  R  D  B  O  A  T  🏠  A  🏠
  🏠  N  Y  E  V  R  U  S  🏠  O  T  🏠  🏠
  L  I  O  P  E  N  🏠  L  🏠  O  J  N  O
  I  M  🏠  E  G  B  🏠  E  C  E  A  🏠  F
  G  R  E  E  N  🏠  E  F  F  E  C  T  C
  H  A  R  K  R  R  O  I  L  K  K  N  A
  T  W  I  🏠  T  🏠  W  C  J  Y  B  E  R
  🏠  🏠  F  E  L  🏠  I  🏠  N  A  U  P  D
  T  T  O  L  L  🏠  C  O  O  K  I  E  S
  S  N  O  M  M  O  C  F  O  🏠  L  L  O
  A  D  🏠  F  A  R  M  🏠  S  I  T  S  🏠
  🏠  E  H  T  F  O  R  E  K  A  E  P  S
```

BOATHOUSE	HOUSE OF COMMONS
CLEAN HOUSE	HOUSE-SITS
CLUBHOUSE	[THE] HOUSE THAT JACK BUILT
COURTHOUSE	HOUSE-TO-HOUSE SURVEY
DOGHOUSE	HOUSEWARMING
DOLLHOUSE	HOUSEWIFE
FARMHOUSE	JAILHOUSE
FIREHOUSE	LIGHTHOUSE
GREENHOUSE EFFECT	OPEN HOUSE
HOTHOUSE	OUTHOUSE
HOUSECOAT	PENTHOUSE
HOUSEFLY	ROUGHHOUSE
HOUSEHOLD	SPEAKER OF THE HOUSE
HOUSEKEEPER	TOLLHOUSE COOKIES
HOUSE OF CARDS	TREE HOUSE

19. GET INTO SHAPE

Shaped like a parallelogram, the grid contains the names of distinctive shapes found in math and elsewhere. The hidden message answers the riddle, "The name of which famous New York City place is made up of an arithmetic term and shape?"

```
                              E
                           L  R
                        C  E  A
                     R  C  L  U
                  I  T  O  G  Q
               C  A  C  N  N  S
            T  N  R  I  E  A  M
         E  G  O  H  E  L  I  X
      M  L  S  S  S  T  A  R  S
   O  E  S  P  H  E  R  E  T
   C  Y  L  I  N  D  E  R
   T  D  Q  R  R  U  A
   A  O  V  A  L  P
   G  N  A  L  E
   O  U  R  Z
   N  T  O
   E  I
   D
```

CIRCLE	PRISM
CONE	RECTANGLE
CROSS	SPHERE
CYLINDER	SPIRAL
DONUT	SQUARE
HELIX	STAR
OCTAGON	TRAPEZOID
OVAL	TRIANGLE

20. IT LOOKS LIKE REIGN

Shaped like a king in chess, the grid contains words and phrases associated with royalty. The hidden message answers the riddle, "Why is a king like a 12-inch measuring tool found in a classroom?"

```
            E
          K T A
            I
      H C R A N O M
        C N R H G
        R E A L M
        E I T
    S A D U C H E S S
        Q P R
        E R O
        L I N
        T N E
        S C B
        A E O
      L C R R U
    A C R O W N R
  U P L S L A Y O R T E
  H E R M A J E S T Y R
```

CASTLE	PALACE
COURT	PRINCE
CROWN	QUEEN
DUCHESS	REALM
EARL	ROBE
HER MAJESTY	ROYALS
KING	THRONE
MONARCH	TIARA

21. JUST DESERTS

Shaped like a saguaro cactus, the grid contains things associated with deserts. The hidden message is the punch line to a joke that begins, "How was your family's day trip to the desert?"

```
                M  Y  D  S
             D  H  A  I  D  L
      I  B   K  E  S  R  S  C
      E  E   S  A  H  A  R  A        S  C
      M  D   O  T  G  T  D  N        U  A
      I  O  T  B  U  T  T  E  Y      T  M
      B  U  J  A  U  T  L  I  O   D  I  C  E
      A  I  B  A  R  A  F  O  E  C  N  E  R  W  A  L
         N  D  O  V  N  D  T  S  T  E  H  I  N  C
            K  I  E  E  N  N  T  K  S  W  A
               N  A  V  A  R  A  C  S
               O  T  S  K  S  L
               I  H  O  E  K  T
               P  V  M  T  C  L
               R  A  H  O  O  A
               O  L  E  Y  R  S
               C  L  G  O  B  I
               S  E  O  C  L  T
               O  Y  O  R  R  A
```

ALOE	CARAVAN	OASIS
ARID	COYOTE	RATTLESNAKE
ARROYO	DEATH VALLEY	ROCKS
BEDOUIN	GOBI	SAGUARO
BUTTE	HEAT	SAHARA
CACTUS	LAWRENCE OF ARABIA	SALT LAKE
CAMEL	MESAS	SAND
CANYON	MOJAVE	SCORPION

22. CLOWNING AROUND

Shaped like a person on stilts, the grid contains things associated with a circus. The hidden message names a performer you'll never see in a circus ... his act of dominating a certain lawn weed is just too mild.

```
              D   S   A
              P   N   N
              O
              T   O   T
          E   H   L   A   G
      N   W   O   L   C   D   I
  T           R   A   R           B
  R           S   B   O           A
  A           E   E   B           R
  P       B   S   S   A   N       N
  E       A   G       T   O       U
  Z       N               I       M
  E   I   D               L   L   S
  R   L                       I   T
  I   O   N               T   A   N
  W                               A
  H                               H
  G                               P
  I                               E
  H                               L
  M                               E
  E                               R
```

ACROBAT	HIGH WIRE
BALLOONS	HORSES
BAND	LION
BARNUM	RINGS
BIG TOP	STILT
CLOWN	TENT
ELEPHANTS	TRAPEZE

23. IT ALL ADDS UP

Shaped like a protractor, the grid contains math and arithmetic words. The hidden message answers the riddle, "What do you say to a kid who needs a hint on an addition problem?"

```
            O  C  A  N
         I  G  R  R  I  N  V  S
      E  T  N  E  I  T  O  U  Q  I
      R  O  O  T  Z        Y  X  M  O  X
   R  T  U  E              I  B  S  A
   A  U  M                 R  E  E
L  D  A  M        L  A        H  T  R  H
E  I  L        D  I  V  I  D  E     T  A  S
D  U  E  L  G  N  A  P  R  O  D  U  C  T  A  M
E  S  U  N  E  T  O  P  Y  H  P  S  U  N  I  M
```

ADDS	MATRIX
ANGLE	MINUS
AREA	NUMBERS
AXIS	PRODUCT
DIAMETER	QUOTIENT
DIVIDE	RADIUS
HYPOTENUSE	ROOT
LINE	TOTAL
MATH	ZERO

24. THE WHEEL THING

Shaped like a bicycle, the grid contains words about cycling. The hidden message answers the riddle, "What did the exhausted boy say after changing both flats on his bike?"

```
  I
  F A L L         W H E E L
      A               R
      N P A T C H I
      E               T
    D   C       M   A
  L A       A     T     P I
F L A T       R I D E B U T R
S E A T             S M I R
  B E               P D
```

BELL	RACE
FALL	RIDE
FLAT	RIMS
LANE	SEAT
PATCH	TIRE
PATH	TUBE
PEDALS	WHEEL
PUMP	

25. MIX AND MATCH

Shaped like a shirt and pants, the grid contains 12 pairs of things that are closely related to each other in some way. The things in each pair got even closer now that we've gone and mixed their letters together. To uncover the words, start with the first letter in each scrambled pair below and read every other letter in order to the end. That'll give you the first word. Cross out those letters, and then read the leftover letters in order to get the second word. Blanks have been provided so that you can write in the words to build your word list.

Each word will appear separately, as usual, in the grid. If you need help, the sorted-out word list can be found on page 66. The hidden message will tell you what things we think are the most closely related.

CROENMTORTOEL

_ _ _ _ _ _ _

_ _ _ _ _ _

RSOPCAKCEET

_ _ _ _ _ _

_ _ _ _ _

DEIXNTOISNACUTR

_ _ _ _ _ _ _ _

_ _ _ _ _ _ _

SCTIATTYE

_ _ _ _ _ _ _ _ _

TFAOSOTDE

_ _ _ _ _ _ _ _ _

GTOELEFS

_ _ _ _ _ _ _ _

IWNASSEPCST

_ _ _ _ _ _ _ _ _ _ _

WHIOSPHE

_ _ _ _ _ _ _ _

NBERCAKCLEALCEET

_ _ _ _ _ _ _ _ _ _ _ _ _

WPOLRAKY

_ _ _ _ _ _ _ _

PFAASISL

_ _ _ _ _ _ _ _

ZAORDIIEASC

_ _ _ _ _ _ _ _ _ _ _

```
      I  F  T  A        H  E  E  F
   C  O  N  T  R  O  L  T  L  P  A
A  O  T     S  I  W  A  O        O  O  I
U  D  L     D  E  T  G  M        B  H  L
            C  S  C  E  E
            K  A  N  T  R
                  I
            I  Y  T  D  D
         D  T  T  X  S  O  A
         I  T  E  E  S  N  Z
      C  N  E  C  K  L  A  C  E
      D  O  T  E     C  E  H  T
      E  S  C  I     S  O  C  S
   P  L  A  Y           P  R  A  K
   A  P  U  R           P  S  T  R
A  S  R  R              E  A  O  B
H  S  I  W              N  T  W  S
```

26. PRETTY CHEESY

Shaped like a piece of Swiss cheese, the grid contains the names of different cheeses. The hidden message asks a question about a certain TV celebrity.

```
I   A   L   L   E   R   A   Z   Z   O   M
M   U   E   N   S   T   E   R   S   S   H
T   P   A   N   E   Y           R   A
M   A   R   F   O   B           A   V
O   R   Y   V   E   L   V   E   E   T   A
N   M           R   O   O   O   A   M   R
T   E           C   C   A   V   L   N   T
E   S   E   E   H   C   T   A   O   G   I
R   A   M   O   E   B           Z   R   A
E   N   B   A   D   L           N   R   P
Y   I   G   A   D   U   O   G   O   S   C
J               A   E   H   M   G   W   E
A               R   E   A   B   R   I   E
C   A   N   I   T   N   O   F   O   S   S
K   A   T   T   O   C   I   R   G   S   E
```

BLUE	HAVARTI
BRIE	MONTEREY JACK
CHEDDAR	MOZZARELLA
COLBY	MUENSTER
EDAM	PARMESAN
FETA	PROVOLONE
FONTINA	RICOTTA
GOAT CHEESE	ROMANO
GORGONZOLA	SWISS
GOUDA	VELVEETA

27. I'D LIKE TO POINT OUT ...

Shaped like an arrow, the grid contains things that have points. The hidden message answers the riddle, "What did the female fencer say to her opponent as she jabbed him with her sword?"

```
            P  E  N  C  I  L  S
            E  N  S  P  H  K  E
            R  E  L  L  I  U  Q
            I  E  S  P  A  N  I
            W  D  O  D  D  I  S
            D  L  S  T  A  C  K
            E  E  T  F  L  O  G
            B  B  I  I  N  R  D
            R  A  N  F  A  N  G
   W  O  R  R  A  Y  G  F  I  S  H  H  O  O  K
      A  Y  R  B  O  E  O  L  H  U  D  G  N
         N  E  A  N  R  T  S  O  A  M  I
            T  N  E  M  U  G  R  A  F
            L  T  P  Y  T  N  E
            E  P  S  O  I
            R  N  T
            S
```

ANTLERS	NAILS
ARGUMENT	NEEDLE
ARROW	PENCILS
BARBED WIRE	PINS
BAYONET	QUILL
DART	SKI POLE
FANG	SPEAR
FISHHOOK	STINGER
GOLF TEE	TACK
KNIFE	UNICORN'S HORN

28. SOMETHING IS FISHY

Shaped like a lobster, the grid contains things that live in the water. The hidden message answers the riddle, "What did the kid at the seashore want on his sandwich?"

```
            P  L      C  E
         T  I  A      N  O  S
      U  A  U         K  R  T
      N  B     R  U  A     T  A
   S           T  T  P           L
      N        E  O  L        O
E           A  R  A  Y  E  B           N
   O  C  T  O  P  U  S  K  S  Q  U  I  D
            D  P  T  T  I
M  U  S  S  E  L  I  E  D  O  L  P  H  I  N
            L  R  R  R  P
K  R  A  H  S  D  A  E  H  R  E  M  M  A  H
J           E  N  H  P  O                 L
            B  H  R  W  P
   L  Y     M  A  L  C  F     I  S
   L  E  E  C  I  R  T  C  E  L  E
   H  P  O  L  L  A  C  S  E  A  L
```

CARP	OYSTER
CLAM	PIRANHA
CORAL	PORPOISE
CRAB	SCALLOP
DOLPHIN	SEAL
ELECTRIC EEL	SKATE
HAMMERHEAD SHARK	SNAIL
KELP	SNAPPER
LOBSTER	SQUID
MUSSEL	TURTLE
OCTOPUS	WHALE

29. MAKING DECISIONS

Shaped like a man sticking out his tongue and making a face, the grid contains things you make. The hidden message answers the question, "There's a saying, 'Haste makes waste,' but would you say that's true for bank robbers?"

```
            N Y O F T I
          F C O N T A C T
        T R O U B L E C T
        H E E R D I N N E R
      F R ● B S M M Y C R
      I N ● E Y A E A N L
    O F R I E N D S T O K E I
  N G S C S A D E T O U R T
    T E Y N E V E I L E B
    M T O R M S R M A F K
F O O L O F Y O U R S E L F E
    V A O C Q U W U I I C
  K E R X P G E O T F D
  A Y E N O M E R R Y
        P W A S Y
        W A V E S
```

BELIEVE	MATTERS WORSE
CONTACT	MERRY
[A] DETOUR	MONEY
[A] DIFFERENCE	MY DAY
DINNER	NICE
[AN] EXCUSE	POPCORN
[A] FACE	ROOM
[A] FIRE	SENSE
[THE] FIRST MOVE	[THE] TEAM
[A] FOOL OF YOURSELF	TROUBLE
FRIENDS	WAVES
[A] FUSS	YOUR BED

30. IT'S A PUT-ON

Shaped like a boot, the grid contains things associated with shoes. The hidden message is good advice from a music teacher.

```
                        R  P  L  E  A  Y  S
                        L  E  S  S  A  T  A
                        S  F  F  P  R  R  E
                        R  E  K  A  E  N  S
                        E  N  P  D  O  T  S
                        P  Z  C  R  F  L  N
                        P  O  L  I  S  H  I
                     S  I  R  L  L  T  H  S
                     H  L  I  H  L  O  G  A
                  H  O  S  O  R  E  O  N  C
               S  R  E  T  S  I  L  B  O  C
            N  P  H  H  E  B  C  S  Y  P  O
   S  U  M  T  M  S  N  O  L  L  E     O  I  M
   T  O  T  U  O  A  S  R  L  C  S     B  L  H
   A  O  P  L  L  A  D  N  A  S        W  S  E
   L  E  A  T  H  E  R  L  B           O  E  H
   F  G  C  O  R  N  S  O              C  R  N
```

BALLET SLIPPERS	HEELS	SANDAL
BLISTERS	LACES	SHOEHORN
CLOGS	LEATHER	SLIP-ON
CORNS	LIFTS	SNEAKER
COWBOY BOOTS	LOAFER	SOLE
ESPADRILLE	MOCCASINS	STRAP
FLATS	MULES	TASSEL
GALOSHES	POLISH	ZORI
	PUMP	

31. TOTAL ECLIPSE OF THE MOON

The moon-shaped grid was *supposed* to be filled with words and phrases containing the word MOON, but there's been a total lunar eclipse. As a result, the word MOON, which appears throughout the word list, has completely disappeared from the grid. So, for example, MOONBEAM in the list will appear only as BEAM in the grid. When you're done, the hidden message completes this definition: "The word 'half-moon' can also mean the white part at the ..."

```
            B  Y  E  N  O  H
         F  L  A  H  M  A
      A  S  E  T  A  H
   S  T  O  N  E  A
   K  A  I  B  R
O  L  N  F  V  S
A  A  O  E  H
M  W  S  O  P
F  T  T  I  A
S  N  H  N  P
F  H  G  G  E  S
   U  I  E  R  C
   R  L  N  N  A  S
      A  L  E  P  I  E
      L  R  E  K  A  R
         S  T  R  U  C  K
```

CRESCENT MOON	"MOONRAKER"
FULL MOON	MOONSCAPE
HALF-MOON	MOONSHINE
HARVEST MOON	MOON SHOT
HONEYMOON	MOONSTONE
MAN IN THE MOON	MOONSTRUCK
MOONBEAM	MOONWALK
"MOONLIGHT SONATA"	"PAPER MOON"

32. GREENHOUSE

Shaped like a shamrock, the grid houses the names of plants, foods, and other things that are always or often green. The hidden message contains the names of three famous fictional characters with green skin.

```
                G  M  I
             G  R  N  I  M
          D  R  A  G  O  N  C
          R  A  S  S  E  D  T
          B  P  S  Y  I  B  L
          E  L  V  E  A
    E  H  P        A  I  W        C  U  A
 L  M  K  Y  E        N        A  K  E  V  R
 M  I  E  T  R  T  A  O     C  H  E  E  O  F  L
 G  A  R  D  E  N  E  R  S  T  H  U  M  B  C  E  R
 O  E  A  G  L  A  G     I     S  P  I  N  A  C  H
    A  L  N  E  D        O        G  L  F  D  R
       D  I  C           P        S  N  O
                         E
                      N  A  D
                   I  C  S  H  A
                P  I  C  K  L  E  J
```

ALGAE	LAWN
AVOCADO	LEAF
BEAN	MINT
CACTI	MOSS
CELERY	PEAR
DRAGON	PEAS
EMERALD	PICKLE
GARDENER'S THUMB	PINE
GRAPE	POISON IVY
GRASS	SLIME
JADE	SPINACH

33. STRINGS ATTACHED

Shaped like a kite with a tail, the grid contains things with strings. The hidden message answers the riddle, "What did the frustrated boy say when he quit tying a string around his finger because it never helped him to remember?"

```
                    O
                N   F   J
            A   O   I   E   N
        I   B   M   M   L   Y   A
    P   R   A   H   A   D   O   K   B
R   S   S   L   G   R   A   T   I   U   G
    K   W   L   E   I   R   L   T   V
        Y   O   Y   O   C   L   E
        T   O   B   N   S   U   I
            N   E   E   T   P
            S   A   T   A   T
                N   T   C
                    E
                        T
                            T
                                I
                                    M
```

BALLOONS	MARIONETTE
BANJO	MASK
BEAN	MITTENS
BOWS	PIANO
CAT'S CRADLE	PULL TOY
GUITAR	VIOLIN
HARP	YO-YO
KITE	

34. PLAYING IT SAFE

Shaped like a shield, the grid contains things that protect in different ways. The hidden message tells something the president of the United States promises to do while taking the oath of office.

```
G E R P B I B Y B A B
A N E B U G S P R A Y
S I D R L O C M E T E
M C N C L T O O P A D
A C E T E R N T P R D
S A F E T Y G L A S S
K V G M P D O U R O E
F T E L R N G D W T M
N A H E O L G A Y E C
  O O H O V L N D S
  C L C F L E T N I
    K F V T S S A
    D L E I H S C
      U S T T I
        T O N
```

ARMOR
BABY BIB
BUG SPRAY
BULLETPROOF VEST
CANDY WRAPPER
COAT
COPS

FENDER
GAS MASK
GLOVES
GOGGLES
GUARD
HELMET

LOCK
MOAT
SAFETY GLASS
SHIELD
TEFLON
VACCINE
WALL

35. TIC-TAC-TOE

Shaped to look like a tic-tac-toe board, the grid consists of words and phrases each of which contain the consecutive letters TIC, TAC, or TOE. The hidden message also hides TIC-TAC-TOE in that order.

ANTACID		HERETIC
ANTARCTIC		OBSTACLE COURSE
ATTACK		OPTICIAN
ATTIC		POTATOES
BALTIC AVENUE		STATIC
BE ON YOUR TOES		TACO
BOSTON CELTICS		TACT
CRUSTACEAN		TICKLE
HAYSTACK		VETOED

36. THE GAME'S AFOOT

Shaped like a human foot, the grid contains words and phrases that have something in common. Can you figure out what it is?

First, use the crossword-style clues on the opposite page to come up with the word list. The blanks give the number of letters in each word or phrase, and the word list is in alphabetical order. Then, as usual, find the words in the grid. Can you tell yet how they're alike?

Whether or not you know the answer, the hidden message will reveal what the items have in common. Should you need help, the complete word list can be found on page 66.

```
                        Y
                  A     M     E  L
            L     E     M     C  L
            G     L     A     N  I
      T     R     I     R     A  T
      H     I  M  U  G  N  H  E  H
      E     N  E  S  I  N  P  C  R
   E  A  M  C  H  H  O  L  I  D  A  Y
   S  D  C  H  O  U  N  T  N  N  L  A
   I  Q  O  N  N  A  U  N  T  O  B
   C  U  P  C  A  K  E  P  O  C  A
   R  A  E  D  I  O  T  O  B  E  C
      R  O  E  F  N  M  U  E  S  K
      T  E  R  A  F  S  N  A  A  Y
      E  U  C  R  O  E  D  N  T  A
      R  B  A  R  O  M  E  T  E  R
      S  M  S  E  T  N  D  T  G  D
```

1. Person who makes on-air comments during a ballgame

_ _ _ _ _ _ _ _

2. Place to play behind the house

_ _ _ _ _ _ _ _

3. Instrument mentioned during weather forecasts

_ _ _ _ _ _ _ _ _

4. Small frosted dessert

_ _ _ _ _ _ _

5. Be given another opportunity to succeed

_ _ _   _   _ _ _ _ _ _

_ _ _ _ _ _

6. Music award for rock or rap

_ _ _ _ _ _

7. Dr. Seuss character who stole Christmas

_ _ _ _ _ _

8. Generals' central command post

_ _ _ _ _ _ _ _ _ _ _

9. Thanksgiving or Hanukkah, for example

_ _ _ _ _ _ _

10. Reproduced word for word, as a translation

_ _ _ _ _ _ _

11. Walking instead of going by car

_ _   _ _ _ _

12. Ingredient used in some chili recipes

_ _ _ _ _   _ _ _ _

13. Struck hard, as with a hammer

_ _ _ _ _ _ _

14. When car traffic is often the heaviest

_ _ _ _   _ _ _ _

15. Holy, like a cow in a phrase

_ _ _ _ _ _

16. Put on a happy face

_ _ _ _ _

37. ARE YOU PACKED?

Shaped liked a pull suitcase on wheels, the grid contains things you might pack for a Florida vacation. The hidden message tells you what you should do with both your suitcase and your vacation.

```
        B  T  R
        A     Y
        T     W
        H     A
        I     T
T  O  S  U  N  S  C  R  E  E  N
B  M  O  C  G  T  H  P  T  J  S
E  H  A  C  S  M  K  A  A  A  U
A  S  A  H  U  A  N  S  R  C  N
C  U  I  S  I  K  N  M  E  K  G
H  R  M  H  T  E  U  D  M  E  L
T  B  C  O  S  U  N  H  A  T  A
O  H  P  R  N  P  H  I  C  L  S
W  T  N  T  A  E  S  K  C  O  S
E  O  S  S  Y  O  Y  U  C  A  E
L  O  M  A  G  A  Z  I  N  E  S
   T                       N
```

BATHING SUIT	MAKEUP	SUN HAT
BEACH TOWEL	MONEY	SUNSCREEN
CAMERA	SANDALS	TANK TOP
COMB	SHORTS	TOOTHBRUSH
JACKET	SOCKS	T-SHIRT
MAGAZINES	SUNGLASSES	WATCH

38. I STRAIN

The I-shaped grid contains words and phrases in which I is the only vowel. The hidden message is one critic's opinion of the puzzle. (We hope it's not yours!)

```
M  I  S  S  I  S  S  I  P  P  I  H  C
F  I  R  S  T  I  N  N  I  N  G  I  T
B  I  G  B  I  R  D  J  I  N  X  H  I
         W  H  I  K  I
         T  H  I  C  K
         I  B  I  I  T
         N  I  W  T  N
         P  R  I  S  M
         I  D  I  P  S
         C  T  L  I  K
         N  N  V  L  I
         I  K  I  L  N
         C  M  S  Z  T
         M  I  I  T  I
S  T  F  I  H  S  T  H  G  I  N  T  I
N  K  K  W  I  N  D  C  H  I  L  L  S
H  S  I  R  I  G  N  I  T  H  G  I  F
```

BIG BIRD	JINX	SKINTIGHT
BIKINI	KILT	SPILL
CHIP	LIPSTICK	STRICT
DIPS	MISSISSIPPI	THICK
FIGHTING IRISH	NIGHT SHIFT	TWIN
FIRST INNING	NITWIT	VISIT
HISS	PICNIC	WIND CHILL
ICING	PRISM	ZINC
	SKIM MILK	

39. WALL-DONE

Shaped like a mirror, the grid contains things you might find on a wall. The hidden message is a comment about Humpty Dumpty.

```
            S  H  T
         L  P  H  H  U
      I  F  L  I  E  S  M
   A  H  P  A  T  R  L  Y  W
N  A  C  S  Q  N  M  T  V  S  W
E  D  T  I  U  R  O  D  B  E  U
S  P  I  D  E  R  M  A  N  M  S
K  I  W  R  T  E  E  H  G  I  E
C  C  S  O  T  P  T  T  I  H  L
O  T  T  U  C  A  E  E  S  C  I
L  U  H  T  A  P  R  W  T  O  T
C  R  G  L  L  L  T  N  I  A  P
A  E  I  E  E  L  S  O  X  F  F
   S  L  T  N  A  N  N  E  P
      T  H  D  W  E  W  A
         L  A  R  U  M
            R  L  L
```

CALENDAR	MURAL	POSTER
CHIMES	NAILS	SHELVES
CLOCKS	OUTLET	SPIDER-MAN
DIRT	PAINT	THERMOMETER
EXIT SIGN	PENNANT	TILES
FLIES	PICTURES	WALLPAPER
LIGHT SWITCH	PLAQUE	

40. HOW DOES YOUR GARDEN GROW?

Shaped like a watering can, the grid contains things that grow in gardens. The hidden message is a plea to a security guard from would-be shoppers at a gardening store right at closing time.

```
    I  F              B  Y  Y  O
 U  C  Y  A           R  H  E  R  R  C
 C  H  A  R  D        A  S  P  A  R  A  G  U  S
 O  T  M  A  E  S     T  I  L  M  N  U        A
    L  S        L  Q  Z  O  D  K  E  E  L  P     E
                E  U  M  A  P  S  L  I  U        P
                C  A  R  R  O  T  F  M  P  E
                O  C  T  S  K  R  N  L  P  A
                T  H  O  R  H  B  A  O  K  R
                A  I  A  S  E  E  E  W  I  S
             L  T  N  A  L  P  G  G  E  N  N  E
             T  O  I  A  T  U  C  A  R  T  I  O
             E  P  K  I  Y  E  L  S  R  A  P  N
```

ASPARAGUS	PARSLEY
BEAN	PARSNIP
BEET	PEAS
CARROT	POTATO
CAULIFLOWER	PUMPKIN
CELERY	RADISH
CHARD	ROSEMARY
EGGPLANT	SAGE
KALE	SQUASH
LEEK	TOMATO
OKRA	YAMS
ONION	ZUCCHINI

41. BACK TO THE DRAWING BOARD

Shaped like a canvas on an easel, the grid contains things you draw. The hidden message answers the riddle, "Why was the female gunslinger good at art?"

```
        Y  B  E  S  T  R  A  W  S  C  D  A  U
        K  A  S  N  E  R  I  F  Y  M  E  N  E
        N  E  W  I  O  U  T  L  I  N  E  S  C
        A  E  R  A  H  C  T  O  C  S  P  O  H
        L  H  A  T  D  R  N  E  I  A  B  W  E
        B  C  A  R  T  O  O  N  R  L  R  A  E
        S  Q  O  U  U  W  I  I  C  A  E  D  R
        C  W  K  C  O  D  S  N  L  R  A  T  S
        S  H  P  I  C  T  U  R  E  Y  T  E  D
           A           L           H
           M           C           R
           B  A  S  E  O  N  B  A  L  L  S
           A  A        O           W  T
           T           C           O
           H           L
```

A MAP	[THE] CURTAINS
AWAY	[A] DEEP BREATH
[A] BASE ON BALLS	ENEMY FIRE
[A] BATH	[A] HOPSCOTCH AREA
[A] BLANK	LOTS
CARDS	NEAR
[A] CARTOON	[AN] OUTLINE
CHEERS	[A] PICTURE
[A] CIRCLE	[A] SALARY
[A] CONCLUSION	STRAWS
[A] CROWD	[A] SWORD

42. PANDEMONIUM

Every item in the word list contains the letters PAN in consecutive order. When these letters appear in the dustpan-shaped grid, they have been replaced by a ⌣, so whatever you do, don't ⌣IC! The hidden message tells what some people with strange tastes might like to eat for breakfast.

```
                    S  G
                    M  I
                    A  A
                    R  N
                    T  T
                    Y  ⌣
          C  S  S  ⌣  D  E  X  I
       ⌣  O  ⌣  J  T  A  E  ⌣  D  I
          S  M  A  P  S  ⌣  M  U  S  H
       O  I  ⌣  M  R  W  I  S  A  E  ⌣  L
       E  E  I  N  O  T  T  U  B  C  I  ⌣
       S  S  O  D  ⌣  ⌣  S  T  A  I  A  S
    E  A  N  N  D  E  S  L  K  O  ⌣  ⌣  N  M
    C  H  I  M  ⌣  Z  E  E  E  M  S  A  Y  A
 R  Z  W  I  R  E  H  T  ⌣  K  N  I  P  ⌣  R  L
 A  M  A  R  O  ⌣  E  H  T  N  I  H  S  A  L  F
```

CHIMPANZEE	PANELS
COMPANION	PANIC BUTTON
DUSTPAN	PANORAMA
FLASH IN THE PAN	PANSIES
FRYPAN	PINK PANTHER
GIANT PANDA	PROPANE
HISPANIC	SMARTY-PANTS
JAPANESE	SPANDEX
PANAMA CANAL	TIMPANI
PANCAKE	WINDOWPANE

43. ALL SMALL

Shaped like a magnifying glass, the grid contains things that are always or often small—some of which could be seen more easily through a magnifying glass. The hidden message answers the riddle, "What do Munchkins do when they chitchat?"

```
                E  R  O  P
             T  D  Y  S  N  A  I  L
          M  I  G  U  B  Y  D  A  L  T
          C  R  H  E  S  A  Y  M  H  L
       E  A  G  E  N  E  T  B  I  K  E  S
       D  R  I  B  G  N  I  M  M  U  H  A
       A  W  S  M  A  E  B  L  I  R  A  E
       L  E  A  R  P  L  U  G  I  T  P  P
          P  L  R  E  P  T  M  O  A  E
          A  R  F  F  A  P  M  W  L  L
          K  I  T  T  E  N  B  K
             N  S  Y  B
             T  E
             P  O
             I  F
             H  A
             C  N
             O  E
             R  E
             C  D
             I  L
             M  E
```

ATOM	EYE OF A NEEDLE	LADYBUG	PORE
BABY	FLEA	MICROCHIP	PRINT
DICE	GENE	PAWN	SHRIMP
DUST MITE	GERM	PEAS	SNAIL
DWARF	HUMMINGBIRD	PEBBLE	STAPLE
EARPLUG	KITTEN	PILLS	THIMBLE

54

44. GET THE MESSAGE?

Shaped liked a sign, the grid contains ways of getting across a message. To get the hidden message, you'll need to use a secret code. (Okay, it's not so secret.) Each letter in the message represents the letter that comes immediately before it in the alphabet. So B becomes A, C becomes B, and so forth, up to Z becomes Y. We hope you get the message, which was written by Benjamin Franklin.

```
U  I  T  S  G  F  K  F  P  M  N  B  E
C  Z  E  L  F  N  N  F  S  H  E  T  Q
O  S  L  A  N  G  I  S  E  K  O  M  S
U  B  E  T  F  P  W  X  D  N  D  N  O
R  S  P  P  O  S  T  C  A  R  D  Y  E
I  E  A  S  T  V  A  D  R  F  F  R  M
E  U  T  J  G  B  S  U  A  X  U  O  A
R  E  H  T  L  B  K  E  H  H  P  T  I
R  B  Y  E  E  I  Y  D  C  S  F  S  L
            L  W  O
            L  R  C
            B  I  T
            O  T  E
            A  I  R
            R  N  C
            D  G  E
            S  E  S
            F  B  E
```

BILLBOARDS	LETTER	SKYWRITING
BROCHURE	MEMO	SMOKE SIGNALS
CABLE	NOTE	STORY
CHARADES	PHONE	TELEPATHY
COURIER	POSTCARD	TV AD
E-MAIL	POSTER	WINK
FAXING	SECRET CODE	

45. FLAG DAY

The flag-shaped grid contains words and phrases found in the first verse of the U.S. national anthem. The hidden message answers the riddle, "What would happen if the Incredible Hulk's alter ego were covered in constellations?"

```
                                              S
    R  H  R  E                          B  E
    O  D  B  E  N  E  S  T           M  R  P
    C  T  H  I  D  R  H  H  G  E  O  G  O  I
    K  T  G  A  A  G  S  A  T  B  A  L  A  R
    E  H  S  T  I  L  L  T  H  E  R  E  D  T
    T  G  S  R  R  L  S  A  P  A  N  A  E  S
    S  I  B  G  A  L  E  E  R  F  E  M  V  D
    B  L  A  N  D  R  U  D  C  E  E  I  A  E
    B  Y  T  W  I  L  I  G  H  T  S  N  W
    A  L        B  U  R  S  T  I  N  G
    Y  R              N  N  E
    L  A
    D  E
    U  S
    O  N
    R  W
    P  A
    R  D
```

BOMBS	LAND
BRAVE	NIGHT
BRIGHT	PROUDLY
BROAD	RED GLARE
BURSTING	ROCKET'S
DAWN'S EARLY LIGHT	STARS
FREE	STILL THERE
GALLANTLY	STRIPES
GLEAMING	TWILIGHT'S
HAILED	WAVE

46. NOW WE'RE COOKING!

Shaped like a hand-held electric mixer, the grid contains utensils used in the kitchen. The hidden answer completes this line said by a carrot: "When I'm out by myself, I always think clearly ..."

```
                    S  N  A  P
              B  R  E  D  N  A  L  O  C
        S  P  O  O  N        U  A  U  T  I  L
        I  E                 T  N  T  L  A  W
        F  E           B  S  T  O  P  A  L  H  O
        T  L  K  N  I  F  E  E  N  D  P  I  D  B
        E  E  E  R  K  R  O  F  L  I  S  P  G  E
        R  R  E  T  T  U  C  E  I  K  O  O  C  T
                    A  S  G  N  O  T  L
                             A
                             T
                             O
                             M
                             A
                          L  S  M
                          I  H  X
                          E  E  D
                          U  R  P
```

BOWL	PLATTER
COLANDER	POTATO MASHER
COOKIE CUTTER	POTS
FORK	SIFTER
KNIFE	SPATULA
LADLE	SPOON
PANS	TONGS
PEELER	WHISK

47. QUICKLY!

Shaped like a stopwatch, the grid contains words and phrases about being in a hurry. The hidden message answers the riddle, "How do you describe a dynamite expert who's intense and in a hurry?"

```
                D   A   S   H
    Y                   Y   K                           E
        R           R   P   E   H               L
            R   R   E   P   D   S   G   D
        O   U   U   O   A   A   M   W   A   G
        H   I   L   C   N   D   A   N   M   O
    G   W   L   A   T   S   D   K   T   E   A   R
    T   A   H   U   S   T   L   E   S   K   L   A
    G   I   F   I   N   I   E   H   A   I   L   C
    T   U   E   O   P   E   H   A   F   L   O   E
        O   D   V   L   K   S   S   L   N   U
        B   O   L   O   A   U   T   U   U   T
            S   C   A   M   P   E   R   R
                S   A   S   T
```

DASH	PUSH
"DON'T DAWDLE!"	RACE
"FAST!"	RUN LIKE MAD
GALLOP	RUSH
GO ALL OUT	SCAMPER
HURRY	SCOOT
HUSTLE	SCURRY
MAKE HASTE	SKEDADDLE
"MAKE IT SNAPPY!"	TEAR
"MOVE IT!"	WHIP

48. TAKE A PEAK

Shaped like a mountain, the grid contains things associated with mountains. The hidden message answers the riddle, "What did the detective say to a crowd as he was chasing a criminal up the mountain?"

```
                    E
                 D  K  O
              S  A  I  S  S
              E  N  H  N  R
           P  D  N  O  O  E  T
           W  N  W  T  W  I  O
        C  R  A  G  S  B  C  R  R
        S  Y  V  T  M  O  A  A  U
        E  P  A  I  E  A  L  R  P
     I  I  M  L  R  I  R  G  F  H  Y
     G  K  C  A  A  R  D  F  H  I  O
  A  S  C  E  N  T  T  I  O  A  L  D  Y
  N  P  O  H  C  I  L  N  D  S  L  E  T
  M  A  R  T  H  C  R  G  A  G  T  L  I
  L  G  S  C  E  N  I  C  V  I  E  W  S
```

ALPS	RIDGE
ANDES	ROCKIES
ASCENT	SCENIC VIEWS
AVALANCHE	SNOWBOARDING
CLIFF	SNOWCAP
CLIMB	T-BAR
CRAGS	TRAM
GAPS	UPHILL
GLACIERS	WATERFALL
HIKE	YETI
PEAK	YODEL

49. STEP LIVELY

This puzzle shows you a game that you can play with one or more friends. First, think of a word, any word, and say it. The next person then says a word he thinks of when he hears that word. The next person then says a word that the last word reminds him of, and so on. The game can continue as long you like. At the end, you may want to see if you can recall the entire chain from start to finish.

In this puzzle, our "free association" chain starts with FOOTBALL, goes to TOUCHDOWN, and leads one step at a time to the final word FIELD, which could then suggest FOOTBALL, as in football field, bringing the chain full circle.

Since the chain is a series of steps that lead from one to the next, the grid is shaped like a set of steps you might walk up. The hidden message is our advice on how to solve the puzzle.

1. FOOTBALL
2. TOUCHDOWN
3. LANDING
4. AIRPLANE
5. BIRD
6. FLAMINGO
7. FLORIDA
8. BEACH
9. UMBRELLA
10. RAIN
11. WIND
12. TORNADO
13. WIZARD OF OZ
14. MOVIE
15. POPCORN
16. BUTTER
17. MILK
18. CEREAL
19. WHEAT
20. FIELD

P
O L
P A J
C N D E
O D R I B
R I U V R W
N N W O S O I
W G I M D D L Z
O G N I M A L F A
D T D L W I N E D R
H B E A C H L R I O D
C I T E S R E K O F T O
U M B R E L L A B T O O F
O E R E T T U B T I P B Y O
T S T C E A I R P L A N E P Z

50. MAKING A CHANGE

Shaped like a light bulb, the grid contains things you change or that are changed. The hidden message answers the riddle, "Why does it take two dummies to change a light bulb on the ceiling?"

```
            S  E  C  A  L  P
         O  N  E  D  T  O  U  H
      D  E  N  I  T  U  O  R  C  O
   L  L  N  D  T  S  H  T  E  B  K  U
   A  C  D  I  R  E  C  T  I  O  N  S
   N  L  L  B  M  A  O  B  C  T  D  A
   E  N  D  O  O  T  U  N  H  I  T  P
   S  E  L  Y  T  S  R  I  A  H  L  A
      E  T  S  O  H  S  P  N  A  R
         O  V  U  N  E  M  N  S
            O  T  R  O  S  E
            I  S  A  F  O  L
            C  T  E  H  D  S
            E  T  S  I  H  E
            S  S  E  S  L  D
               T  B  T  O
               A  D  O  D
               E  M  R  J
               R  Y
```

[YOUR] ATTITUDE	LANES
BOYS' VOICES	LUCK
CHANNELS	MENU
[YOUR] CLOTHES	[YOUR] MIND
[THE] COURSE OF HISTORY	[YOUR] MOOD
DIAPERS	PLACES
[YOUR] DIET	PLANS
DIRECTIONS	[YOUR] ROUTINE
HAIRSTYLES	SEATS
JOBS	[YOUR] SHOES

51. WIN-WIN SITUATION

Shaped like a sports trophy, the grid contains things you win. The hidden message completes an often-misquoted phrase by football coach Vince Lombardi who said, "Winning isn't everything ..."

```
              B   U
              T
              T
              D   E   E
  N   G   B       T   N   E   V   E       P   W   L
  E       A   A   N   L   B   B   S   M   R       A
  P       T   M   T   O   G   I   A   A   I       D
  O       T   S   E   T   N   O   C   T   Z       E
  S       L   N   Y   T   I   E   G   I   E       M
  U   U   E   T   M   E   L   E   C   T   I   O   N
      P   O   M   R   L   E   R   L   N
          E   A   Y   E   I   U   E
          T   R   O   P   H   Y   D
          G   B   S   N   W
              O
              T   S   W
          I   N   C   I   L
          D   R   A   W   A
      S   A   P   P   R   O   V   A   L
```

APPROVAL	EVENT	RACE
AWARD	GAME	SPELLING BEE
BATTLE	GRAMMY	SUPER BOWL
CASE	LOTTERY	TITLE
CONTEST	MEDAL	TONY
DEBATE	MEET	TRIP
DUEL	MONEY	TROPHY
ELECTION	OSCAR	U.S. OPEN
	PRIZE	

52. START AT THE END

Shaped like a dartboard with a big bull's-eye in the middle, the grid contains 20 words that each start and end with the same letter. For variety's sake, each word begins with a different letter of the alphabet. The hidden message puts three other such words together to tell you what you get if you have the smallest Eskimo canoe in a place where you wash.

```
            R  T  I  N
         D  E  I  E  P  S  G  T
      E  A  R  T  H  Q  U  A  K  E
      R  R  B  A  F  F  U  L  F  B
   O  T  T  I  C  K  E  T  L  L  Y  S
   L  E  B  A  L     H  O  W  U  A
   E  K  O  O  K     B  P  H  C  P
   O  M  A  X  I  M  U  M  I  E  K  S
      T  R  L  E  U  B  T  N  W  Y
      K  D  A  O  R  C  E  G  Y  A
         C  A  T  H  O  L  I  C
            K  N  A  X
```

ALOHA	MAXIMUM
BLOB	NEON
CATHOLIC	OLEO
DARTBOARD	PULL-UP
EARTHQUAKE	REAR
FLUFF	SPAS
GALLOPING	TICKET
HITCH	WHEW
KOOK	XEROX
LABEL	YUCKY

53. LET'S CALL IT A DAY

Shaped like the sun, the grid contains things kids often do during the course of a day. The hidden message is a parent's reminder of one more thing for you to do.

```
                    A
    V               E                   R
       I         S  N  M  D           E
          D  D  L  L  E  A  R  N  D  A
          S  E  E  F  R  I  E  N  D  S
          E  K  O  E  L  L  S  O  N  T
       P  F  R  W  G  E  N  S  K  L  A  W
 H  A  N  G  O  U  T  A  T  M  A  L  L  O
       R  H  W  G  C  V  M  U  G  W  E  H  C  E
       S  T  E  K  L  E  G  E  A  T  O  B
       R  M  O  U  H  S  K  K  H  P
       Y  O  O  U  O  E  R  T  L  E
       H  H  C  N  U  L  T  A  E  A
    C            P  S  E  Y           T
    S            E                    T
                 H
```

CHEW GUM	READ
DRESS	SCHOOL
EAT LUNCH	SEE FRIENDS
E-MAIL	SHOWER
HANG OUT AT MALL	SLEEP
HOMEWORK	SNACK
LAUGH	TALK
LEARN	VIDEOGAME
LEAVE HOUSE	WAKE UP
PLAY	WALK

14. ANIMAL HUNT WORD LIST

1. acroBAT
2. bookWORM
3. CATnap
4. COWlick
5. CROWbar
6. FISHy
7. FLYer
8. GOOSEbumps
9. hot DOG
10. leapFROG
11. LION's share
12. outFOX
13. PIGtails
14. RAT race
15. RAY gun
16. sawHORSE
17. TIGER woods
18. TOADstool

25. MIX AND MATCH WORD LIST

CONTROL REMOTE [remote control]
DINOSAUR EXTINCT
GOLF TEES
INSECT WASPS
NECKLACE BRACELET
PASS FAIL
ROCKET SPACE
STATE CITY
TASTE FOOD
WISH HOPE
WORK PLAY
ZODIAC ARIES

36. THE GAME'S AFOOT WORD LIST

1. annOUNCEr
2. backYARD
3. baroMETER
4. CUPcake
5. get a SECOND chance
6. GRAMmy
7. grINCH
8. headQUARTers
9. holiDAY
10. LITERal
11. on FOOT
12. PINTo bean
13. POUNDed
14. rush HOUR
15. sACREd
16. sMILE

1. PUT ON A HAPPY FACE

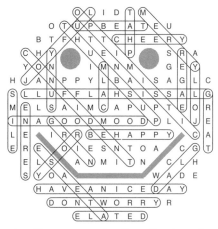

I doubt the saying "happy as a clam" applies to a clam in chowder.

2. OPEN FOR BUSINESS

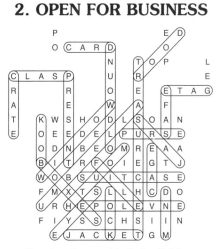

People who need bait for fishing.

3. WHAT AN ICE GAME

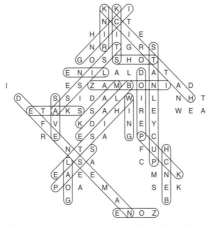

The goalie didn't wear a face mask. [It hadn't been invented.]

4. PLUG IT IN

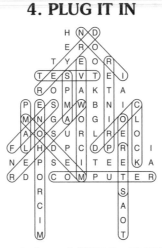

He took a big gulp instead. [GULP = PLUG backwards.]

5. I NEED THIS RIDE NOW!

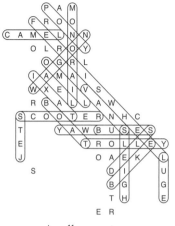

A roller coaster.

6. NEW YORK, NEW YORK

"... it's commonly called 'the city that never sleeps.'"

7. AW, NUTS!

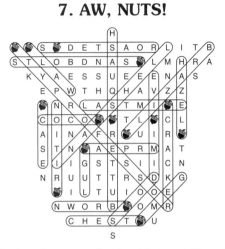

"... it makes sense that 'nut' is in nutritious."

8. LOSER!

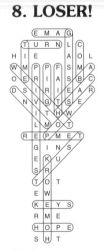

He lost interest.

9. GET A LOAD OF THIS!

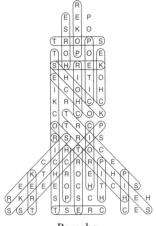

Porsche.

10. LISTEN UP

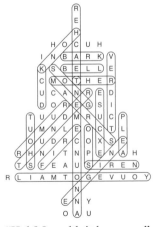

"Huh? I couldn't hear you."

11. ON THE GO

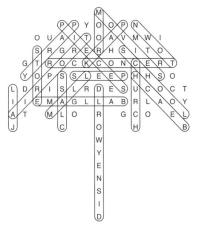

You might go directly to Go.

12. SOFT IN THE HEAD

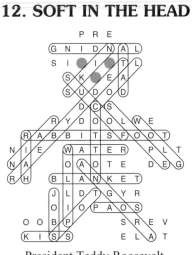

President Teddy Roosevelt.

13. THREW AND THREW

Judo opponents are like small problems: Don't let them throw you.

14. ANIMAL HUNT

A bat boy sat on a cuckoo clock on Fox TV.

15. FLOATING AWAY

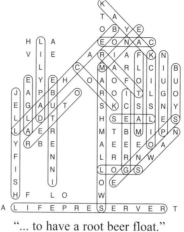

"... to have a root beer float."

16. IT'S A GIFT!

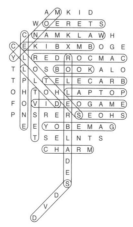

A kid who gets a lot of presents.

17. TAKE FIVE

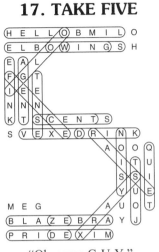

"Oh, some G-U-Y."

[G, U, and Y are the missing initial letters in the word list.]

18. PUT YOUR HOUSE IN ORDER

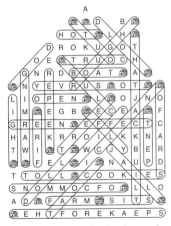

A housebroken dog broke into a house.

19. GET INTO SHAPE

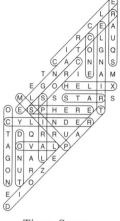

Times Square.

20. IT LOOKS LIKE REIGN

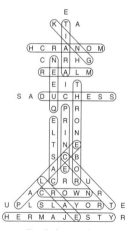

Each is a ruler.

21. JUST DESERTS

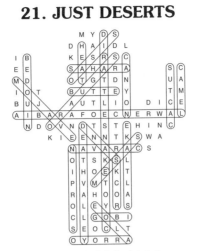

"My dad liked it, but I didn't think it was so hot."

22. CLOWNING AROUND

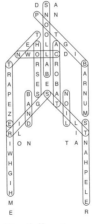

Dandelion tamer.

23. IT ALL ADDS UP

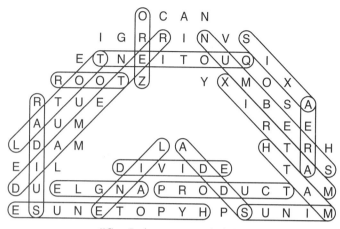

"Can I give you sum help?"

24. THE WHEEL THING

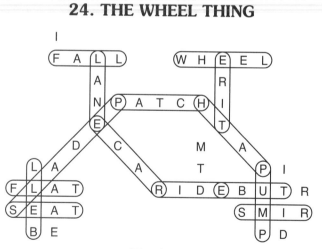

"I'm tired!"

78

25. MIX AND MATCH

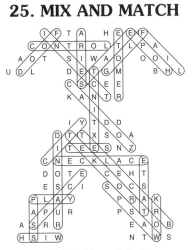

That would be kids and their parents.

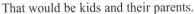

26. PRETTY CHEESY

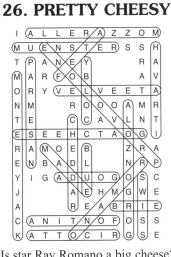

Is star Ray Romano a big cheese?

27. I'D LIKE TO POINT OUT ...

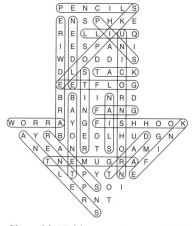

She said, "Did you get my point?"

28. SOMETHING IS FISHY

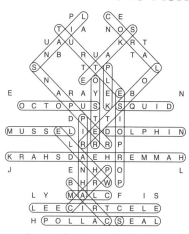

Peanut butter and jellyfish.

29. MAKING DECISIONS

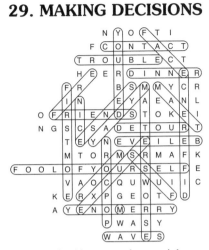

Not if they're looking to make a quick getaway.

30. IT'S A PUT-ON

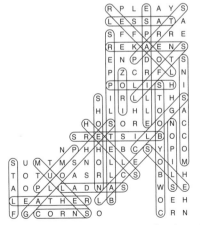

"Play a French horn but not a shoehorn."

31. TOTAL ECLIPSE OF THE MOON

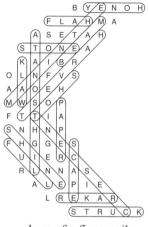

... base of a fingernail.

32. GREENHOUSE

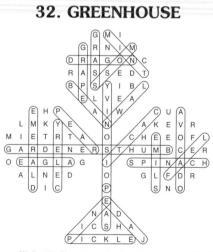

[The] Incredible Hulk, Kermit the Frog, and [the] Grinch.

33. STRINGS ATTACHED

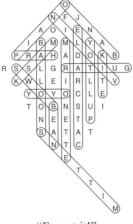

"Forget it!"

34. PLAYING IT SAFE

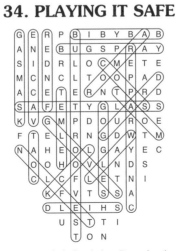

Protect and defend the Constitution.

35. TIC-TAC-TOE

I got TICked off when a pisTAChio nut fell on my big TOE.

36. THE GAME'S AFOOT

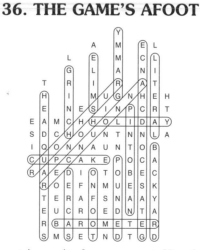

All the items contain a unit of measurement. [See the word list on page 66 to find out what each one is.]

37. ARE YOU PACKED?

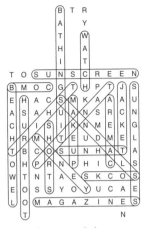

Try to pack as much in as you can.

38. I STRAIN

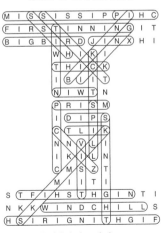

I think it stinks.

39. WALL-DONE

Humpty wasn't weird, but he was off-the-wall.

40. HOW DOES YOUR GARDEN GROW?

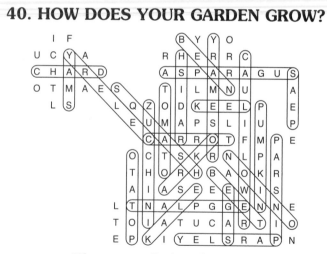

"If you carrot all, please lettuce in."

41. BACK TO THE DRAWING BOARD

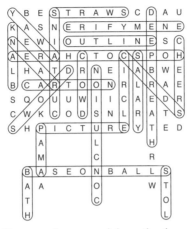

Because she was quick on the draw.

42. PANDEMONIUM

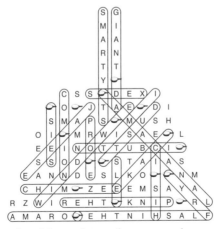

Spanish omelets and some marzipan.

43. ALL SMALL

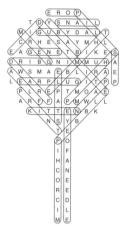

They make small talk.

44. GET THE MESSAGE?

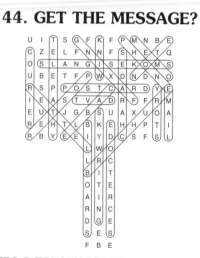

UISFF NBZ LFFQ B TFDSFU JG UXP BSF EFBE, which becomes
"Three may keep a secret if two [of them] are dead."

45. FLAG DAY

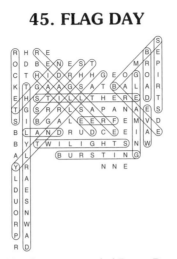

He'd be the star-spangled Bruce Banner.

46. NOW WE'RE COOKING!

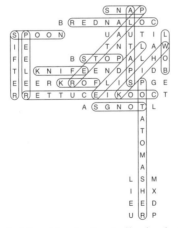

"... but in a blender I get all mixed up."

47. QUICKLY!

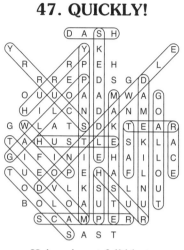

He's going at full blast.

48. TAKE A PEAK

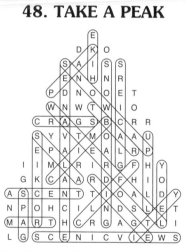

"Don't worry. I'm right on his trail."

49. STEP LIVELY

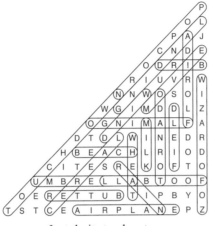

Just do it step by step.

50. MAKING A CHANGE

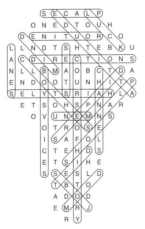

One to hold the bulb, and one to rotate the ladder.

51. WIN-WIN SITUATION

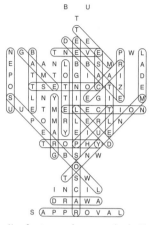

"... but wanting to win is."

52. START AT THE END

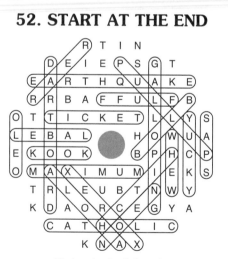

Tiniest bathtub kayak.

53. LET'S CALL IT A DAY

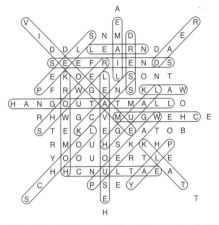

"And don't forget to brush your teeth!"

Index

Italics indicate answer page number

All Small 54, *88*

Animal Hunt 22, *73*

Are You Packed? 48, *85*

Aw, Nuts! 15, *70*

Back to the Drawing Board 52, *87*

Clowning Around 31, *77*

Flag Day 56, *89*

Floating Away 24, *74*

Game's Afoot, The 46, *84*

Get a Load of This! 17, *71*

Get Into Shape 28, *76*

Get the Message? 55, *88*

Greenhouse 42, *82*

How Does Your Garden Grow?

.... 51, *86*

I'd Like to Point Out 37, *80*

I Need This Ride Now! 13, *69*

I Strain 49, *85*

It All Adds Up 32, *78*

It Looks Like Reign 29, *76*

It's a Gift! 25, *74*

It's a Put-On 40, *81*

Just Deserts 30, *77*

Let's Call It a Day 65, *93*

Listen Up 18, *71*

Loser! 16, *70*

Making a Change 62, *91*

Making Decisions 39, *81*

Mix and Match 34, *79*

New York, New York 14, *69*

Now We're Cooking! 57, *89*

On the Go 19, *72*

Open for Business 10, *67*

Pandemonium 53, *87*

Playing It Safe 44, *83*

Plug It In 12, *68*

Pretty Cheesy 36, *79*

Put On a Happy Face 9, *67*

Put Your House in Order 27, *75*

Quickly! 58, *90*

Soft in the Head 20, *72*

Something Is Fishy 38, *80*

Start at the End 64, *92*

Step Lively 60, *91*

Strings Attached 43, *83*

Take a Peak 59, *90*

Take Five 26, *75*

Threw and Threw 21, *73*

Tic-Tac-Toe 45, *84*

Total Eclipse of the Moon 41, *82*

Wall-Done 50, *86*

What an Ice Game 11, *68*

Wheel Thing, The 33, *78*

Win-Win Situation 63, *92*

• • •

About the Author

Mark Danna earns his living writing puzzles: more than 20 word search books; the newspaper-syndicated, rhymes-with-clues *Wordy Gurdy*; American Mensa's annual page-a-day calendar *365 Brain Puzzlers*; and some 200 crosswords, including Sundays in *The New York Times*. Danna has been an associate editor at *Games* magazine and a staff writer for *Who Wants to Be a Millionaire*. To order personalized word searches, crosswords, or other puzzles, contact Mark at puzzlestogo@gmail.com.

Also by Mark Danna

Amazing Word Search Puzzles for Kids
Brain Aerobics: Word Search Puzzles
Fantastic Word Search Puzzles for Kids
Great Word Search Puzzles for Kids
Large Print Word Search Puzzles
Large Print Word Search Puzzles 2
Petite Elegant Word Searches
Scattergories Word Search Puzzles
Word Search Puzzles to Keep You Sharp